LOOK CLOSER

SHORELINE

PHOTOGRAPHED BY
FRANK GREENAWAY
OF THE NATURAL HISTORY MUSEUM, LONDON

WRITTEN BY
BARBARA TAYLOR

DORLING KINDERSLEY • LONDON • NEW YORK • STUTTGART

DK

A DORLING KINDERSLEY BOOK

Editor Sue Copsey **Art editor** Val Wright
Senior editor Christiane Gunzi **Designer** Floyd Sayers
Design assistants Nicola Rawson, Lucy Bennett
Production Louise Barratt
Illustrations Nick Hall
Index Jane Parker
Managing editor Sophie Mitchell
Managing art editor Miranda Kennedy
Consultants
Geoff Boxshall, Barry Clarke, Theresa Greenaway,
Gordon Howes, Tim Parmenter, Edward Wade, Kathie Way

With special thanks to Robin James, Mike Quorm, and
all the staff of Weymouth Sea Life Centre, and to
Mark Jones for supplying some of the animals in this book.

Endpapers photographed by Jules Cowan, Bruce Coleman Ltd.

First published in Great Britain in 1993 by
Dorling Kindersley Limited
9 Henrietta Street
Covent Garden
London WC2E 8PS

A CIP catalogue for this book is available from the British Library.
ISBN 0 7513 5038 9

Colour reproduction by Colourscan, Singapore
Printed and bound in Italy by New Interlitho, Milan

CONTENTS

Look for us, and we
will show you the size
of every animal and
plant that you read
about in this book.

LIFE ON THE SHORE

WHERE THE LAND MEETS the sea, and forms sandy or rocky shores, all kinds of wildlife make their homes. Many crabs, worms, fish, and plants have adapted to life in this salty environment, where there is little fresh water. Some shoreline plants and animals live so close to the sea that the tide washes over them twice a day. They have to be able to survive in both wet and dry conditions. Today, shorelines all over the world are threatened by pollution from oil spills, factory waste, and litter left by people. We need to keep our beaches clean and remember that we share them with the wildlife that lives there.

Queen scallop
Chlamys opercularis
shell 9 cm wide
LIVES IN NORTH-
WESTERN EUROPE

Hermit crab
Pagurus bernhardus
body 10 cm long
LIVES IN EUROPE, NORTH
AMERICA, AND SCANDINAVIA

Tub gurnard
Trigla lucerna
30 cm long
LIVES IN EUROPE

Peacock worm
Sabella pavonina
body 26 cm long
LIVES IN EUROPE

Lesser weever fish
Trachinus vipera
12 cm long
LIVES IN EUROPE AND
NORTH AMERICA

King ragworm
Nereis virens
30 cm long
LIVES IN NORTH AMERICA,
NORTHERN EUROPE, AND
NORTH-EAST ASIA

Common lizard
Lacerta vivipara
15 cm long
LIVES IN CENTRAL AND
NORTHERN EUROPE, AND
NORTHERN ASIA

Oystercatcher
Haematopus ostralegus
43 cm long
LIVES IN EUROPE, INDIA,
NORTH-WEST AFRICA,
SCANDINAVIA, AND THE
MIDDLE EAST

Thrift
Armeria maritima
flower stem 9 cm high
flower 1.5 cm wide
LIVES NORTH OF
THE EQUATOR

Natterjack toad
Bufo calamita
6 cm long
LIVES IN EUROPE

Sea pea
Lathyrus japonicus (maritimus)
flower stem 10 cm high
flower 1.5 cm wide
LIVES IN NORTH AMERICA, NORTHERN
ASIA, AND NORTHERN EUROPE

WRIGGLING WORMS

THESE KING RAGWORMS get their name from the ragged fringe of flat legs, called parapodia, along the sides of their bodies. Ragworms often live in burrows beneath the surface of the sand, and they wriggle about to keep a current of water flowing past. This contains oxygen, which a ragworm needs in order to breathe. The water also carries scents and tastes from above the sand. When the ragworm senses prey, it shoots out of its burrow to grab it. In the breeding season, female king ragworms lay eggs on the sea bed, and the males fertilize them. Then all the adults die. Their eggs develop into tiny larvae which swim around, feeding on plankton, while they grow and develop. After about two years, they will be fully grown adults, living in the sand.

GUESS WHAT?
These animals are called king ragworms because they can grow so large. An adult may be up to 90 cm long, and wider than a ruler.

TINY TENTACLES
Each body segment has a pair of flat, paddle-like parapodia. The ragworm uses these for crawling, swimming, and breathing. They work like the gills of a fish to take in oxygen from the water. Each one has two small, feeler-like cirri, and two bundles of stiff bristles, for gripping surfaces.

These iridescent violet colours are made by light reflecting off both sides of the worm's thin skin.

The body is made up of more than 100 segments.

FOOD DETECTORS
On the ragworm's head there are many sense organs. These help the worm to hunt for food, and pick up information about its environment. The four eyes, two palps, and two short antennae are sensitive to light, smell, and touch. There are also four tentacles which can feel things.

SHRINKING WORM
To escape from enemies, such as birds, the king ragworm contracts (tightens) the muscles that run from its head to its tail. This makes its body much shorter, so the ragworm can move backwards suddenly, or disappear into its burrow quickly.

These two short antennae, and the two palps, help the worm find food. The mouth is on the underside of the head.

If king ragworms lose their tentacles, they can grow new ones.

PINCER POWER
The king ragworm is an omnivore, which means that it feeds on almost anything it can find, such as fish eggs, larvae, and plant and animal remains. This animal is a fierce hunter, seizing prey with its strong, pincer-like jaws. There are six to ten teeth on each jaw.

The bristles on the parapodia can spread out like a fan to help the worm grip the sand and mud.

The worm's body is flat, so it can crawl into cracks and under stones, and slide through the sand easily.

MOBILE HOME

THIS BRIGHTLY COLOURED hermit crab rips its food apart with its sharp pincers. Hermit crabs are scavengers, feeding mainly on the remains of dead animals. They crawl around on the shoreline, pulling themselves along with the strong front legs that stick out of their shell. A hermit crab does not have a hard outer layer on its abdomen (the rear part of the body) as most crabs do. So it finds an empty shell, such as this whelk shell, to live in. As the hermit crab grows bigger, it changes its shell for a larger one. Hermit crabs come out of their shells to mate. Then the female carries her eggs around with her inside the shell until they hatch. The tiny larvae join the mass of plankton floating and feeding near the surface of the sea. Several weeks later they sink to the sea bed, where they search for a small, empty shell to use as their first home.

GUESS WHAT?
If the hermit crab damages one of its legs, it sheds it and grows a new one in its place.

A FOOT IN THE DOOR
If the hermit crab is attacked by an enemy, such as a sea bird, it quickly pulls itself deep inside its shell. Then the crab wedges the larger of its two front pincers across the opening of the shell. This seals off the entrance, like an armour-plated door.

These legs end in sharp claws for gripping on to the sea bed.

The crab's outer skin, called the exoskeleton, is hard at the front to protect the exposed parts of the body.

Each eye is on the end of a long stalk.

The hermit crab uses its two front pairs of legs for walking, and drags its home behind it wherever it goes.

These two short feelers, called antennules, are sensitive to touch.

Feathery mouthparts pass small pieces of food towards the mouth.

HITCHING A RIDE
Barnacles, sea anemones, and sponges often live on top of a hermit crab's shell. These animals cannot move by themselves, but the crab carries them around to new feeding areas. In return, they disguise the crab's shell as it moves around on the sea bed. The stinging tentacles of the anemones also help to put off the crab's enemies.

These long, flexible antennae (feelers) smell the water for food.

Close-up, you can see the ragworm inside this hermit crab's shell.

BED AND BREAKFAST
If you look closely, you can see that a ragworm has wriggled up from inside the hermit crab's shell to share its meal. This kind of ragworm often lives inside the shells of hermit crabs. Here it does not have to search for food, and it is safe from birds and other enemies.

FISH FINGERS

TUB GURNARDS WALK slowly over the sea floor on their fins. They use the finger-like rays at the front of their pectoral fins to push themselves along. These fish usually live in small groups, called schools, in shallow water near the shore. Here they search for food amongst the sand, mud, and pebbles. Tub gurnards eat many kinds of small fish, as well as shrimps, crabs, and sea-dwelling worms. In summer, each female gurnard lays thousands of tiny eggs that measure less than a millimetre across. At first, the young which hatch out of the eggs float in the water close to the surface. But here they are easy prey for larger fish. So when the surviving young are fully developed, they swim down into deeper water to begin their adult lives.

GUESS WHAT?
Gurnards get their name from the French word "grogner", which means "to grunt". This is because of the loud grunting noises that these fish make to keep in touch with each other.

COLOUR CHANGE
This young tub gurnard's pectoral fins have blue edges and bright blue spots on them. As the fish grows larger, these striking colours will change. A fully grown tub gurnard has brilliant red and blue pectoral fins with green edges.

The fish uses these large pectoral fins for balancing and turning.

The pointed snout is a good shape for scooping up food from the sea bed.

The dorsal fin stands up to keep the fish steady in the water.

Mottled brown colours help the fish to blend in with the sand and shingle of the sea floor.

The tail fin pushes the fish through the water.

There are no scales on the head. Instead, it is protected by small, bony plates and spines.

FEELING FINS

The three rays at the front of each pectoral fin work rather like feelers. The tub gurnard uses them for walking, and for poking about for food on the sea bed. They are separate from the rest of the rays on the fin, which are joined together by a thin, webbed skin, called a membrane. Each of the front rays can move on its own, in the same way as your fingers.

A sensitive organ, called the lateral line, runs down each side of the body. This detects movements in the water.

Like all fish, the gurnard breathes through gills. These are under the bony gill covers on each side of the head.

A fish's eyes do not have eyelids. Instead, the sea water keeps them moist and clean.

If danger threatens, the pectoral fins flick sand and gravel over the body, to hide it.

A PLACE IN THE SUN

COMMON LIZARDS CAN slip easily through clumps of grass on the shore, hunting for insects and spiders to eat. Like all reptiles, lizards need to be warm in order to move around, and they often stretch out on the sand to bask in the sunshine. Winter is too cold for them, and food is short, so they find a sheltered place, such as a burrow, where they can hibernate (sleep). In spring, common lizards form pairs for mating. The female finds a damp place in the sand and lays 4 to 11 eggs, which are protected by a transparent (see-through) membrane. The young soon hatch and run around, feeding on spiders and insects, such as flies. The adults take little interest in their young, and many of them are eaten by snakes, birds, or mammals.

An eyelid wipes over each eye from time to time, to keep it clean.

The colours and patterns on the lizard's scales help to hide it from both predators and prey.

Like most reptiles, lizards shed their skin in order to grow.

The lizard's nostrils are on the tip of its snout.

Strong jaws for grabbing prey

SIXTH SENSE

The common lizard belongs to a group of animals called reptiles. Like most animals, reptiles can see, hear, feel, taste, and smell. They also have a forked tongue, which picks up chemical information from the air. A special organ in the roof of the mouth uses the information to build up an image of the animal's surroundings. This organ is called the Jacobson's organ.

GUESS WHAT?
Unlike most reptiles, this lizard's young are fully formed by the time it lays the egg sacs. Instead of a hard shell, they only have to break out of a thin, bag-like membrane.

Close-up, you can see a small ear opening on the side of the head.

The long, thin body slides easily through grass and under pebbles.

QUICK AS A FLASH

The common lizard chases prey among the sand dunes until it gets very close. Then at the last moment, it darts forward to seize the animal in its strong jaws.

A LUCKY BREAK

If an enemy grabs the lizard's tail, it has a very useful trick for escaping. It simply breaks off part of its tail and runs away. There are special weak points in the tail, so it does not hurt if it breaks off. A new tail gradually grows, although it does not have weak points like the old one.

Lizards have good eyesight, and they can see in colour.

These long, strong toes grip surfaces well. Lizards are good at climbing.

Most of the bones in the tail can break apart easily, allowing the lizard to escape from a predator's grip.

The tail is often longer than the body. The lizard uses it for swimming, and to help balance its body when it is running or climbing.

A FOREST OF FANS

AT LOW TIDE, PEACOCK worms look like tiny, muddy pipes sticking out of the beach. But when the tide comes in and covers them with water, beautiful feathery fans spread out from the ends of each tube. These fans are the gills of the peacock worm. The worm's soft body is hidden inside its long, protective tube, which it builds from mud and sand. Each tube sticks up about 10 cm above the sand, but there may be another 40 cm hidden below. The animal's body is divided into hundreds of segments, like the body of an earthworm. In spring and summer, peacock worms release many tiny eggs into the water. These eggs hatch into larvae, which drift in the sea with the plankton. After about two weeks they settle down on the shore, where each one builds a tube to live in.

GUESS WHAT?
This worm's fan of gills looks rather like a peacock's fan of tail feathers. That is why these worms are known as peacock worms.

The gills are for breathing, as well as for catching food.

The worm makes its tube from mud and sand, cemented together with mucus.

The gills sense movements in the water, and changes in light and dark.

FOOD FAN
The feathery gills catch tiny water creatures and scraps of food floating past in the water. Each gill pushes food towards the worm's mouth, which is at the centre of the fan. The gills also trap tiny particles of sand and mud.

The worm's mouth is hidden in the centre of its gills.

In times of danger, and when the tide is out, the worm pulls its head and gills back inside the tube.

MUD AND SLIME
A peacock worm builds its smooth, rounded tube out of tiny pieces of mud and fine sand. It sticks them together with a slimy substance called mucus, which it makes inside its body. The tube is lined with mucus, so that the worm can slide up and down easily.

Close-up, you can see fringes of tiny hairs, called cilia. These help to trap food, and move it towards the mouth.

The fan is divided into two semi-circles. Each of these has between 8 and 45 gills.

The gills can be all sorts of colours, such as brown, red, or purple. They usually have darker bands of colour running through them.

LYING LOW
Peacock worms are usually covered by water. When they are exposed to the air at low tide, the worms go down to the bottom of their tubes. Here they stay cool, damp, and safe from enemies.

The lower end of the tube is usually fixed to pebbles beneath the sand. This keeps it firmly in place when the sea washes over it.

BURIED ALIVE

IN CLEAR, SHALLOW water close to the shore, the lesser weever fish lies waiting for a meal to pass by. It often lies almost buried, with just its eyes, mouth, and poisonous dorsal fin poking out of the sand or shingle. This means that the fish can see, catch food, and defend itself, with most of its body hidden. In summer, the weever fish moves up and down the shore as the tide goes in and out. It spends winter in deeper waters, further out to sea, where it can avoid the rough waves which bad weather brings to the coast. The female weever spawns (lays her eggs) in summer. Each tiny egg has a number of yellow oil droplets inside, which help to stop it sinking. After about ten days, the eggs hatch into young which float in the sea with the plankton. When the young are fully developed, they leave the surface of the sea and swim down to the sea floor.

STINGING FINS
If the weever is alarmed, or attacked by an enemy, such as a flatfish, it raises the fan-like fin on its back. This fin, called the dorsal fin, is supported by several sharp spines. At the base of these spines there are sacs of poison. If the weever needs to defend itself, it injects poison into the enemy through its sharp spines.

Mottled yellow and brown colours on the body blend in with the sea floor. This helps the fish to hide from enemies and prey.

These rounded side fins, called pectoral fins, are for pushing and steering the fish through the water. They also dig holes in the sea bed.

This long fin along the back is supported by about 25 bony rays.

SANDY SECRETS
The weever fish digs itself a shallow dip in the sea bed with the fins at the front of its body. It also blows sand out of the way with the water that passes out of its gills. Then it lies in wait, ready to ambush prey, such as shrimps, shore crabs, and worms.

GUESS WHAT?
Sometimes people tread on weever fish buried beneath the sand of the seashore. If the poisonous spines on the dorsal fin pierce a person's skin, they cause a painful sting.

WATER WORKS
Like all fish, the weever breathes through gills. These work like our lungs to take in oxygen from the water. The weever opens and closes its mouth all the time, drawing in water to push over its gills. Then it forces the water out again, past the bony gill covers on each side of the head.

Overlapping scales cover and protect the body. They are thin, light, and flexible, so that the fish can move easily.

Spines on this small black fin inject poison into attackers. The poison runs along grooves in the spines.

The large mouth sweeps upwards out of the sand and gravel to catch food. It also gulps down water for breathing.

A bony cover, called the operculum, protects the delicate gills underneath.

PIED PIPER

THE OYSTERCATCHER'S loud, piping call, and
black and white feathers make it easy to find on the
shoreline. As the name suggests, oystercatchers feed
mainly on oysters and other molluscs, but they also
eat small crabs, shrimps, and worms. In autumn and
winter, these birds live in large groups, called flocks.
In spring and summer they form pairs and choose a
small area on the shore, called their territory. A
female lays two to four eggs in a shallow hole called
a scrape. The male and female take it in turns to sit
on the eggs, which hatch after about four weeks.
The chicks can run around soon after hatching, but
they rely on their parents to feed them for
several weeks, or even months.

GUESS WHAT?
Sometimes the two halves
of a sea creature's shell
may shut tightly, trapping
an oystercatcher's bill
before it has managed to
break the shell apart. The
bird can only get free by
cracking the shell against
a stone until it opens.

SPOT THE EGG
The colours and patterns on the
oystercatcher's eggs make them
look like pebbles, so they are
difficult for enemies to spot.
Oystercatchers sometimes try to
fool an enemy by getting off
their eggs and pretending to sit
on them somewhere else.

*The nostrils are high
up, so they do not
become clogged with
sand when the bird is
digging for food.*

*The tip of the
bill is narrow
and strong, for
prising the two
halves of a
shell apart.*

*The feet spread
wide so that the
oystercatcher does
not sink as it walks on
wet sand and mud.*

*The speckled eggs
blend in well with the
pebbles, which
makes it difficult for
enemies to find them.*

A SMASHING BILL

An oystercatcher's long, blunt bill is specially adapted for breaking open shells. It levers them off rocks, and prises or smashes them open. When the bird finds an open shell, it pushes its bill between the two halves and cuts the muscle which holds them together. If the shell is closed, the bird hammers away at one side with its bill until it breaks through to the soft flesh inside.

A thick covering of waterproof feathers on the body keeps it warm and dry.

NOISY NEIGHBOURS

During the breeding season, oystercatchers become very noisy, as each pair claims its own territory on the shore. All the birds rush around with their bills pointing down towards the ground, making shrill piping calls. These loud messages warn other birds to keep away.

An animal with patches of two or more colours, like the oystercatcher, is called "pied".

The tail feathers help the oystercatcher to steer in the air. They also balance the weight of the bird's body when it perches or sits on the ground.

SHARING THE SHORE

An oystercatcher is just one of the many kinds of birds which poke about on the shoreline looking for food. Each kind of bird has a different size or shape of bill, so that it can find food at different depths in the mud or sand. In this way, the birds share the rich food supply, and many different kinds of birds can live close together.

TOAD IN THE HOLE

DURING THE DAY, the natterjack toad stays inside its sandy burrow. When night falls, the toad creeps out of its hiding place to hunt for insects in the cool, damp air. Natterjack toads hibernate (sleep) during the cold winter months, burying themselves deep in the sand. In spring they migrate to fresh water nearby, where they breed. The males croak loudly to attract females. After mating, the females lay strings of eggs about two metres long in the water. Each string contains up to 4,000 eggs. Five to ten days later, tadpoles hatch out of the eggs and swim around, feeding mainly on algae (simple plants). After six to eight weeks they have changed into tiny toads measuring less than one centimetre long. Now they are ready to leave the fresh water and begin life on the shore. It will take four or five years for these young toads to become fully grown.

GUESS WHAT?
Toads can survive away from water for much longer than frogs. But their skin can easily dry out, so they stay cool below the surface of the sand during the day.

HUNGRY HUNTER
Natterjack toads feed mainly on insects, especially ants and beetles. They have huge appetites, and may eat hundreds of insects in one night. The toad flicks out its tongue at an insect, catching it on the sticky tip. As the toad swallows the prey, it blinks. This forces its eyes down into the head, and helps to push food down the throat.

PEELING OFF
The natterjack toad breathes through its skin as well as with its lungs, so it is important that the skin stays in good condition. Like frogs and other amphibians, the toad moults (sheds its skin) every five or six days. It peels off the old skin with its mouth and front feet, to reveal a shiny new skin underneath. Natterjack toads usually eat their old skin.

LITTLE LEGS
Natterjack toads have much shorter back legs than most other toads and frogs. They cannot swim or jump as well as their relatives, but they are surprisingly nimble, and are good at walking and running.

Natterjack toads are sometimes called golden backs, because of this narrow yellow line along the back.

Bulging eyes give the toad a wide field of vision.

Nostrils for taking air into the lungs

Strong front legs for burrowing into the sand

The toes are webbed and widely splayed. This is a good shape for shovelling sand.

DO NOT DISTURB

If the natterjack toad spots a predator, such as a bird, it can puff up its body and straighten its back legs to make itself look taller, fatter, and fiercer. This is often enough to stop the animal attacking the toad. But if a predator does grab it, a foul-tasting poison oozes out from the parotoid glands behind its eyes. Most animals quickly drop the toad and look for a tastier meal instead.

A round, flat eardrum on each side of the head picks up sounds.

These large lumps are parotoid glands full of poison, which oozes out if an enemy attacks the toad.

Patterns and bumps on the skin help the toad to blend in with its sandy surroundings.

SEASIDE FLAPPERS

QUEEN SCALLOPS LIVE in large groups, called colonies. They live on the sea bed, close to the shore, where they feed on tiny sea plants. These animals are much better swimmers than other shelled sea creatures, such as mussels. They flap along through the water in a series of jerks. The two halves of a scallop's shell are called valves. They are strong and hard, and protect the soft body inside. In summer, female scallops release clouds of eggs into the water. A tiny larva hatches out of each egg, and swims around for about three weeks. Then it anchors itself to a surface, such as a piece of seaweed, with strong threads that it produces inside its body. About a year later, when the shell is fully developed, the scallop swims off to join a colony of adults.

WATER JETS

Scallops swim by opening and shutting the two halves of their shell, rather like clapping. This forces water out behind them in a strong jet, pushing them forwards through the water. When danger threatens, queen scallops can shoot backwards rapidly to escape.

The streamlined shape of the shell cuts through the water easily. This means that the scallop can quickly swim away from a lurking starfish.

These ridges running across the shell can tell you how old the scallop is.

Scallops swim by clapping the two valves of their shell.

About 20 broad ribs fan out from the bottom of the shell to make it extra strong.

Starfish like to eat scallops. They are strong enough to pull the two valves apart to reach the soft body inside.

The two parts of the shell are called valves. They are joined together with a strong elastic substance, called ligament.

SEAFOOD SUPPER

Queen scallops lie on the sea floor with their shells open, waiting for food to float past. They trap tiny plants, called algae, in the waving hairs on their gills. These hairs work rather like a sieve to filter food from the water.

Barnacles often grow on top of scallop shells. They help to disguise the scallops as they lie on the sea bed.

GUESS WHAT?
Sea creatures which live in shells are often called shellfish. But they are not related to fish. Scallops are molluscs, and are related to the slugs and snails that you may find in the garden.

A WRINKLY QUEEN
As the soft body of the queen scallop grows, its shell gets bigger too. The speed at which the shell grows depends on certain things, such as changes in temperature. This speeding up and slowing down causes ridges on the shell, which are rather like the rings in a tree trunk. You can count these ridges to find out the age of a scallop. Queen scallops can live for up to eight years.

These tiny, sensitive tentacles can sense enemies, such as starfish.

These rows of small, simple eyes can sense moving objects, and changes in light and dark.

The mottled colours of the shell blend in with the sand and gravel. This makes it difficult for enemies, such as sea birds, to spot the scallop.

A SPLASH OF COLOUR

IN SUMMER, SEA PEAS and thrift bring patches of bright colour to the shoreline. These plants grow among the rocks and pebbles on the shore, and are able to survive the salty spray blowing in from the sea. Many shoreline plants, like thrift and sea peas, have long roots to reach the rainwater that trickles between the pebbles and collects underground. These plants grow low on the ground, out of the wind. But thrift flowers have long stems, so when the wind blows, it shakes out the seeds. They fall to the ground and grow into new plants somewhere else along the shore.

Paper-thin sepals and delicate, leaf-like bracts protect each flower.

LEAFY CUSHIONS
The leaves of thrift grow in a low, grass-like cushion. Close to the ground, the plant can survive the constant buffeting of sea winds. The cushion also traps moisture, so any water vapour that escapes from the leaves is less likely to be blown away by the wind.

GUESS WHAT?
These plants look small because we can only see the part that is above ground. But thrift roots can grow to more than one metre long, and the creeping stems of a sea pea plant can be up to 80 cm long.

The thrift's narrow leaves grow close to the ground, where they are protected from the wind.

FUNNY FLOWER
A sea pea flower is an unusual shape. It has a large petal at the top and a smaller one on either side. There are two more petals at the bottom which protect the pollen sacs and the female parts of the flower.

Sea pea flowers look similar to sweet pea flowers.

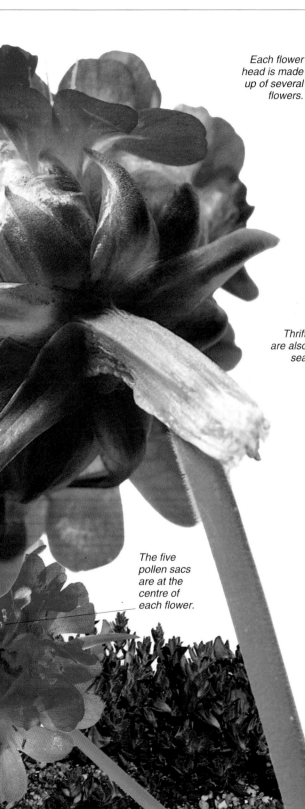

Each flower head is made up of several flowers.

Thrift plants are also called sea pinks.

The five pollen sacs are at the centre of each flower.

INDEX

GLOSSARY

Abdomen *the rear part of the body*
Algae *simple plants such as seaweeds*
Antennae *a pair of feelers*
Barnacle *a small, shelled, sea-dwelling animal that attaches itself to rocks, plants, and other objects*
Bivalve *a mollusc, such as a scallop, which has a two-part, hinged shell*
Cilia *short, hair-like threads*
Exoskeleton *a tough covering on the body, made of a substance called chitin*
Gills *organs that animals such as fish use to take in oxygen from the water*
Gland *an organ that produces a chemical substance*
Hibernate *to rest or sleep during the cold months of the year*
Iridescent *shimmering with colour, caused by light reflecting off two surfaces*
Larva *the young, grub-like stage of an animal, such as an insect*

Lateral line *the line of sensitive cells along each side of a fish's body*
Migrate *to travel long distances to find food and a suitable place to breed*
Mollusc *a soft-bodied animal, such as a slug or snail, which often has a shell*
Mucus *a slimy, often poisonous substance that certain animals produce*
Omnivore *an animal that eats both plants and other animals*
Operculum *a protective cover, such as a fish's gill cover*
Parapodia *pairs of simple walking legs*
Pied *having two or more colours, usually black and white (animals)*
Plankton *tiny, floating sea creatures and plants*
Sepal *one of the outer parts of a flower which protects the bud*
Tentacles *flexible feelers for touching, feeding, or smelling*